Dear Parent:

Congratulations! Your child is taking the first steps on an exciting journey. The destination? Independent reading!

STEP INTO READING® will help your child get there. The program offers five steps to reading success. Each step includes fun stories and colorful art. There are also Step into Reading Sticker Books, Step into Reading Math Readers, Step into Reading Write-In Readers, Step into Reading Phonics Readers, and Step into Reading Phonics First Steps! Boxed Sets—a complete literacy program with something for every child.

Learning to Read, Step by Step!

Ready to Read   Preschool–Kindergarten
• **big type and easy words** • **rhyme and rhythm** • **picture clues**
For children who know the alphabet and are eager to begin reading.

Reading with Help   Preschool–Grade 1
• **basic vocabulary** • **short sentences** • **simple stories**
For children who recognize familiar words and sound out new words with help.

Reading on Your Own   Grades 1–3
• **engaging characters** • **easy-to-follow plots** • **popular topics**
For children who are ready to read on their own.

Reading Paragraphs   Grades 2–3
• **challenging vocabulary** • **short paragraphs** • **exciting stories**
For newly independent readers who read simple sentences with confidence.

Ready for Chapters   Grades 2–4
• **chapters** • **longer paragraphs** • **full-color art**
For children who want to take the plunge into chapter books but still like colorful pictures.

STEP INTO READING® is designed to give every child a successful reading experience. The grade levels are only guides. Children can progress through the steps at their own speed, developing confidence in their reading, no matter what their grade.

Remember, a lifetime love of reading starts with a single step!

To Dr. Francine G. Patterson
and the staff of the Gorilla Foundation
and to the staff
of NYZS/The Wildlife Conservation Society,
with thanks for all their assistance

Random House ⌂ New York

Text copyright © 1997 by Joyce Milton. Illustrations copyright © 1997
by Bryn Barnard. All rights reserved under International and Pan-American
Copyright Conventions. Published in the United States by Random House
Children's Books, a division of Random House, Inc., New York, and
simultaneously in Canada by Random House of Canada Limited, Toronto.

Photo credits: Ronald H. Cohn/The Gorilla Foundation, 43;
© Wildlife Conservation Society (Bronx Zoo), 47.

www.stepintoreading.com

Educators and librarians, for a variety of teaching tools, visit us at
www.randomhouse.com/teachers

Library of Congress Cataloging-in-Publication Data
Milton, Joyce. Gorillas : gentle giants of the forest
/ by Joyce Milton ; illustrated by Bryn Barnard.
p. cm. — (Step into reading. A step 3 book.) SUMMARY: Discusses gorillas,
their behavior, and how scientists have studied them.
ISBN 0-679-87284-1 (trade) — ISBN 0-679-97284-6 (lib. bdg.)
1. Apes—Juvenile literature. [1. Gorilla. 2. Apes.] I. Barnard, Bryn, ill. II. Title.
III. Series: Step into reading. Step 3 book.
QL737.P96 M56 2003 599.884—dc21 2002013432
Printed in the United States of America 23 22 21 20 19 18 17

STEP INTO READING, RANDOM HOUSE, and the Random House colophon are
registered trademarks of Random House, Inc.

STEP INTO READING®

STEP 3

GORILLAS
GENTLE GIANTS
OF THE FOREST

by Joyce Milton

illustrated by Bryn Barnard

In the jungle
some workers
are busy
cutting trees.

They don't know it,
but up the hill
a family of gorillas
is taking
its noontime nap.

The biggest gorilla

opens one eye.

He hears the workers' shouts.

Suddenly he jumps up,

slaps his chest,

and lets out a loud scream—

RRRRRR-AAHHHEEE!

That scream is

one of the scariest sounds

in the world.

It says: KEEP AWAY—OR ELSE!

The workers drop their tools

and run for their lives!

A male gorilla
can weigh 500 pounds.
That's more than
twice as much
as a grown man.
The gorilla is also
many times stronger!

He can snap
a tree branch in half
with his teeth.
His arms are long
and powerful.
When he spreads them wide,
they stretch for eight feet.

For a long time
people were afraid of gorillas.
They told stories
of fierce apes
that attacked
anyone who came near.

A few scientists
wondered if
the stories were true.
They decided
to go into the African forests
and see for themselves.

At first the scientists
were afraid.
But they learned
not to show it.
Why?

If you run from a gorilla,

he may chase you and bite you.

But his charge is mostly bluff.

If you meet a gorilla,

you have to stand still

and pretend

you aren't scared.

Then he will

stop charging

and run

right past you.

Dian Fossey
was one of the first
to study wild gorillas.
To make them trust her,
she tried to act
like a gorilla.
She scratched herself
and thumped her chest.
She grunted and chewed leaves.

Once, when a gorilla
charged her,
Dian made an ugly face.
The gorilla
was so surprised
he stopped in his tracks
and sat down.

After a while the gorillas
got used to Dian.
One young male—
Dian called him Peanuts—
was very curious.
He came closer and closer.
Dian stretched out her hand
and lay still.

Very gently
Peanuts touched her fingers.
Dian was so excited
she almost cried.
She was the first human
ever to be touched
by a wild gorilla!

By watching gorillas up close,
Dian and other scientists
found out what they
are really like.

Gorillas are
gentle creatures.
They live quietly
in groups.
The leader
is an older male.
Scientists call him
a silverback.
He gets his name
from the silvery gray hairs
on his back and neck.

Young male gorillas
are called blackbacks.
In the group
they are followers.

When a blackback
is nine or ten years old,
his hair
starts to turn gray.
In a few years
he will become
a silverback.
Then he may
stay with the group
or wander off on his own.

Female gorillas are
half as big as males.
They spend their time
taking care of their babies.
When a baby gorilla is born,
it weighs four or five pounds.
Its skin is smooth
and hairless.

When the group moves
from place to place,
the mother carries her baby
in one arm.

The baby drinks
her mother's milk
and grows strong.
When she is
two months old,
she is ready to ride
on her mother's back.

She holds tight
to the long hairs.
But sometimes
she loses her grip
and falls—OOPS!

This silverback
is leading his group
through the forest,
looking for breakfast.
The gorillas walk
single file
on all fours.
They rest their weight
on the backs of their fingers.
A gorilla can walk
on its hind legs, too.
But only for a few steps.

Soon the gorillas find
a patch of wild celery.
The celery is
fresh and sweet.

Breakfast takes
two or three hours.
Then it is time
for a nap.

In the afternoon
the gorillas will eat
another big meal.
They eat almost all day long.

Gorillas like many kinds
of wild plants.
Bamboo shoots. Ferns.
Tree bark. Wild blackberries.
Even scratchy nettles!

Around noon the group

settles down for a nap.

But one young gorilla

is wide awake

and ready to play.

He puts a leaf

on his head

just for fun.

Then a tiny frog
hops right under
his nose.
He chases after it.

In the trees nearby
a hungry leopard
is watching.
A young gorilla
would make a tasty meal.

Suddenly the silverback
wakes up.
He smells the leopard
and starts to hoot:
HOO—HOO—HOO!

He grabs a leaf
and holds it
between his lips.
When a gorilla does this,
watch out!
It means he is angry!

POK! POK! POK! POK!
The silverback
beats his chest.
Then he rips up
handfuls of grass
and throws them
into the air.
He runs sideways
on all fours.
What is he doing?
He is showing his stuff!
A silverback
will defend his group
to the death.

Even a leopard
won't fight
an angry silverback.
The big cat slinks away
into the forest.

Just before sunset

the silverback

breaks up some bushes

and piles them

around him.

He is making a nest!

All gorillas sleep in nests.
Every night
the young gorillas
build new nests
in the branches of a tall tree.
The older gorillas
are too heavy
to climb trees.
They make their nests
on the ground.
The mothers cuddle
with their babies.

Are gorillas smart?

For a long time

most scientists

didn't think so.

Now a gorilla named Koko

is proving them wrong.

When Koko was a baby,

a scientist named

Penny Patterson

became her teacher.

Penny taught Koko

the same sign language

used by deaf people.

Koko has learned about 2,000 words.

She even makes up new words.

Koko calls broccoli *stink food*.

She calls a mask an *eye hat*.

Koko can do many things
a child can do.
She likes to look
at picture books.
She plays
with her pet dog, Flower.
She is even learning
to read.

But there is one thing
Koko can't do—
she can't talk.
So Penny gave her a computer
that talks for her.
By watching how Koko
uses her computer,
scientists will find out
how all gorillas
think and learn.

Koko at her computer.

No one knows the future
of the wild gorillas.
The African countries
where they live
are poor and crowded.
People need land
for farms and villages.

They are chopping down
the great forests
where the gorillas live.
Many Africans want
to save the gorillas.
But they need help.

Today more than 300 gorillas
live in American zoos.
They mate and have babies
just like wild gorillas.

Omani was born

in a zoo in New York City.

Her mother was born in a zoo, too.

Will Omani's grandchildren

live in zoos?

Maybe not.

Maybe someday the

forests will be saved.

*Omani at
21 months.*

Then Omani's
grandchildren
might live free
in the wild!